REDNECK
HAIKU

MARY K. WITTE

D1281818

SANTA
MONICA
PRESS

811.6
w.t

Published by:
Santa Monica Press LLC
P.O. Box 1076
Santa Monica, CA 90406-1076
1-800-784-9553
www.santamonicapress.com
books@santamonicapress.com

SANTA
MONICA
PRESS

Printed in the United States

Santa Monica Press books are available at special quantity discounts when purchased
in bulk by corporations, organizations, or groups. Please call our Special Sales
department at 1-800-784-9553.

ISBN 1-891661-29-9

Library of Congress Cataloging-in Publication Data

Witte, Mary K., 1949-
    Redneck haiku / by Mary K. Witte.
        p. cm.
    ISBN 1-891661-29-9
    1. Rednecks—Poetry. 2. Haiku, American. I. Title.
PS3623.I88R43 2003
811'.6—dc21
                                        2003000337

Cover and interior design by Ann Buckley

Mom, thanks for everything, especially the neat genes.

Haiku: three line verse,
  five, seven, five syllables,
  captures a moment.

Redneck: person who
  lacks class but enjoys a life
  without rich folks' rules.

Wedding night fireworks
as Flo's ex-husband threatens
to bring back the kids.

Go to the dentist?
Grandpa went once, and now look—
he has no teeth left.

Turkey fryer bought
from cable shopping channel
burns down trailer park.

9

**Betty Lou surprised
to learn you *can* get pregnant
in church parking lot.**

Goat was barbecued

after eating seat covers

in Bubba's new truck.

Bobby learns to read,

sets a family record.

He's only thirteen.

Stored in shirt pocket,

old match stick cleans Jake's ears, comb,

fingernails, and teeth.

Reno is scene of

grandparents' recent wedding.

"About time," kids say.

Mixed emotions date:

   box seat NASCAR race tickets

   with world's biggest geek.

Game warden stops by

to see one tagged, legal deer.

The rest are hidden.

Election crisis:

vote for union Democrat

or black sheep cousin?

Bubba's mobile home
was a tornado target,
now an Allstate claim.

Last Las Vegas trip

spoiled by Granny's indecent

exposure arrest.

Sign "Will work for food"

gets attention at roadside.

"Howdy, Uncle Clyde!"

High school football team
headed for championship
'til deer season starts.

Southern Comfort gone.

Bottoms up; the last goes down.

Pickup veers to right.

Lake patrol fines Jake

for out-of-season fishing,

beer, and dynamite.

When Flo goes to Mom's,
Bubba dines on canned chili,
Pepsi, and Pop Tarts.

RV at Wal-Mart:

  shopping while just passing through

  or putting down roots?

25

Clyde's Vegas winnings

    barely cover truck repairs

    and beer for trip home.

Fireworks wake Grandpa.

Nap disturbed, he shouts curses.

Children laugh and run.

Wanda's new wind chime

made of kitchen utensils

she seldom uses.

Bubba's mom's cookies

buy him perks during his stay

at the county jail.

Garth Brooks look-alike

causes uproar when spotted

at local cafe.

Sundowner Jones is
    named for the place of his birth—
    the drive-in movie.

Engine overheats

as Jake flees highway patrol.

Chug beers or toss them?

Bubba's rear bumper,

trailer, and boat can be found

at bottom of lake.

Favorite "cousins"

at all weddings, births, and deaths:

Jim Beam, Jack Daniels.

Clyde went with cousins

to shoot golf for the first time.

Took his best shotgun.

Spring: Grandpa trades his
winter weight corduroy cap
for summer straw hat.

Bubba's name is sewed

on his uniform shirt and

hand-tooled on his belt.

Interstate rest stop.

Lunchmeat sandwiches, fried pies,

ice cold grape Nehi.

On half his paydays
Jake signs his check over to
Ed's Feed Store and Bar.

Kids toss cherry bombs.

Boat sinks, beer lost, children laugh

'til Pop swims ashore.

Bobby's spring break trip

cost him five hundred dollars

and clinic visit.

Cousin on TV.

Had visit from aliens

and got anal probe.

Clyde's barbecue sauce
   wins prize at county fair but
   was bought at Safeway.

**No wedding complete
without cold beer and Elvis
impersonator.**

New local law bans

outdoor cooking fires, prompting

move to next county.

Jake hunts and fishes
while Wanda drives forklift at
local lumber yard.

Clyde depressed, drinking.
Divorce cost alimony
and NASCAR tickets.

Shrimp and Buffett tunes.

Will this beer last, or do we

need a run to town?

School hot lunch program

shut down after cooks were caught

brewing white lightning.

Turquoise ring Jake bought
at highway truck stop is now
Wanda's wedding band.

Old empty beer cans

found on road and sold for cash

financed keg party.

Cowboy on the ground.

Flash of color over horns.

Thanks, rodeo clown.

Twelve dogs under porch.

Frame collapses; seven die.

Duck blind now pointless.

Clyde's retirement plan:

twenty-five dollars worth of

lottery tickets.

Early spring morning.

Easter Bunny hops in sights.

Tastes great with dumplings.

Bobby Lee's new shirt,

bright orange, real chick magnet,

reads "Wal-Mart Cart Crew."

Bigger house? No, girl.

With this trailer and that barn,

we got lots of room.

Deep in Death Valley,

truck overheats, no water.

Grapes of wrath—again.

Wanda's trip to bar

to break up fight, drag Jake home,

is neighborhood news.

Clyde's Bait Shop beer sales
provide his tow truck business
a steady income.

Flo on winning streak,
    played slots all day and all night,
    fainted from hunger.

Wanda and Jake get

    bargains on Christmas gifts at

    Guns 'n' Gold Pawn Shop.

Bubba's bowling team

   holds record for beer consumed

   and gutter balls thrown.

Big Vegas hotel.

Bell captain sneers at luggage:

plastic Wal-Mart bags.

Pickup, shiny red

in Grandpa's dim memory,

now rusts in tall weeds.

Granny's house settles.

Back door sticks shut. Front door used

first time in ten years.

Pam in county jail

for assaulting coach at son's

Little League ball game.

Bow-hunting season.

Bubba unprepared 'til he

returns to pawn shop.

Grandpa made to sleep
on porch after going back
for seconds on beans.

Chopping enough wood

to keep house warm in winter

keeps Granny busy.

Free casino beer

   led to foolish betting that

      left Clyde broke again.

Broken toys in yard.

Traveling Bible salesman

knows he'll get this sale.

**Cat population
declines after Bobby Lee
gets birthday shotgun.**

Wanda's third wedding

started an hour late to let

best man make beer run.

Plate filled to the max

at all-you-can-eat buffet.

Jake grins: "Life is good."

Custody battle

    drags through court for months over

    truck and hunting dogs.

All Bubba's brothers

chipped in for wide screen TV

for NASCAR season.

77

Thanksgiving turkey

was deep-fried in peanut oil

"As seen on TV."

Clyde's new monster truck

is highway patrol magnet,

also attracts chicks.

Granny told to leave
casino after remarks
offend "stud" players.

Well-dressed trailer trash
will have muumuus and flip-flops
in matching colors.

Rest stop closure sign

panics Wanda on Route One

after large coffee.

**Jake lobbies Congress
for holiday to honor
Petty family.**

Youngest hunting dog

    learns the hard way how to tell

    a skunk from a cat.

Clyde's voice mail greeting:
"If the baby's really mine,
name it after me."

How to celebrate

twenty-five years of marriage?

New hunting rifle.

Ice cold beer goes great
with illegally caught trout
fried with hushpuppies.

Downtown Las Vegas.

Gramps has no luck with hookers

'til he takes a bath.

Jake rode to work with

wet tee-shirt contest winner

'til his wife found out.

Wanda's hip slit skirt

allows her to climb into

monster pickup truck.

July Fourth fireworks

    get hunting dogs stirred up while

    house dog whines in fear.

Family black sheep
recently evicted from
condemned trailer park.

Father's Day neck tie

    replaces missing tent rope

    on last camping trip.

Clyde nears his deadline

on community service

before next court date.

Flo sets fashion at
   trailer park with bouffant hair
   and acrylic nails.

On his first plane ride
Bubba has panic attack
cured by a quick beer.

Grandpa's "attorney,"

the only one he trusts, is

two-barreled shotgun.

Jake's chicken gumbo

looks like muddy swamp water,

was judged best in state.

Grandpa's new young wife
allows moonshine, draws line at
chewing tobacco.

After heavy rain,

    road sign to Bubba's place reads,

    "Road closed—boat required."

Wanda and Flo spend
most Saturday nights playing
Bingo at Elks Lodge.

The biggest trophy

in Clyde's den is for first place

at truck rodeo.

Driving his RV

   in San Francisco gives Jake

      a thrill a minute.

Family in awe:

reunion attended by

high school graduate.

Grandpa feared teeth lost

until dog pulled them from Flo's

backyard compost heap.

Yosemite trip:

Shoot, cook, and eat local deer.

Thousand dollar fine.

Wanda returns to

Laundromat after six-pack.

Where are all her clothes?

Pulsing lights, low hum,
    Granny prays, hunting dogs whine:
    spaceship lands in swamp.

Pam, newly pregnant,

doesn't know which guy to pick

for shotgun wedding.

Rooster crows before

Mom's morning coffee and now

simmers on the stove.

High school career day.

Jake's kids cheer when he arrives
in his garbage truck.

Bubba got divorced,

but children from the marriage

are still his nephews.